INSIDE THIS PLANNER

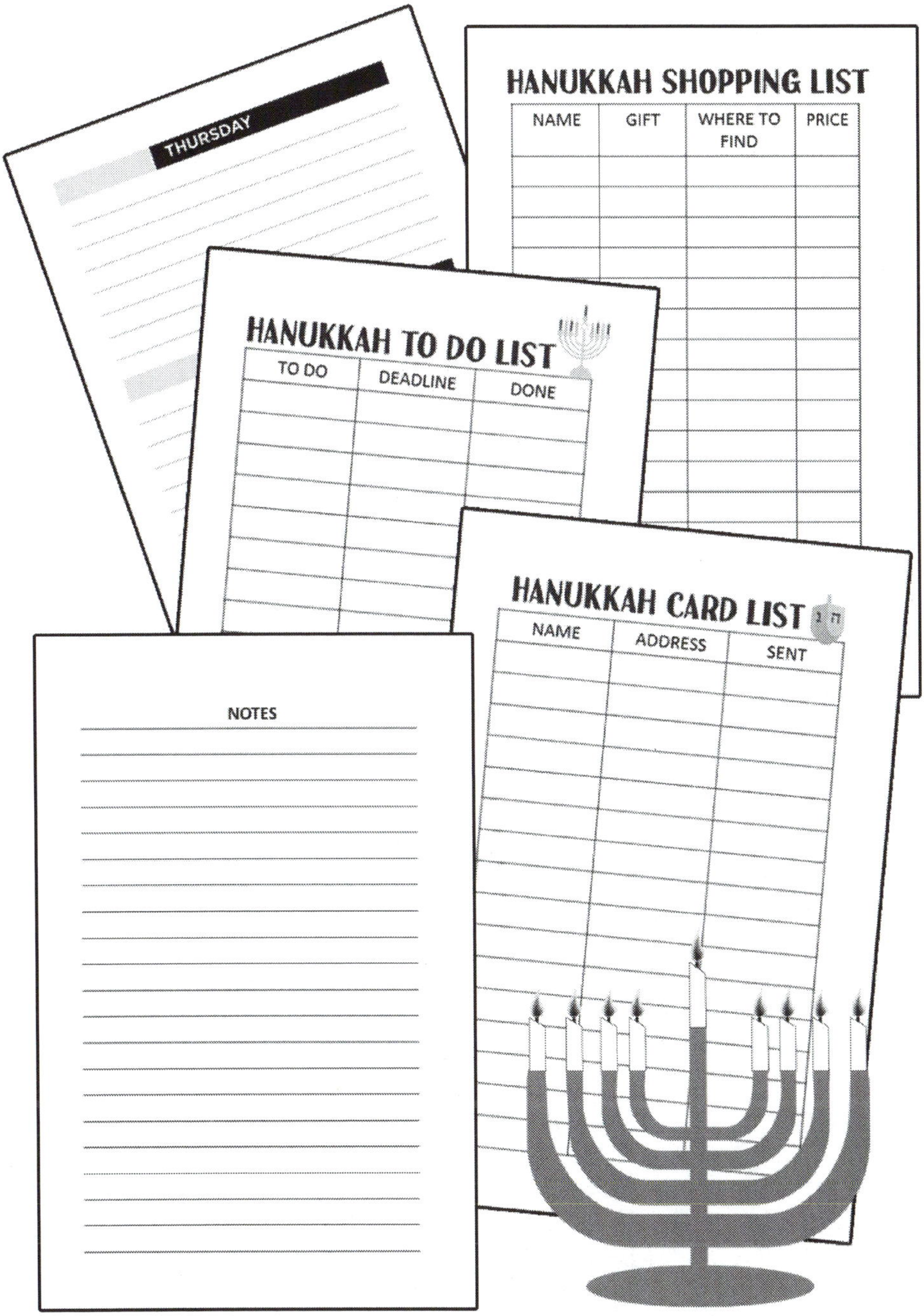

HANUKKAH TO DO LIST

TO DO	DEADLINE	DONE

HANUKKAH TO DO LIST

TO DO	DEADLINE	DONE

HANUKKAH TO DO LIST

TO DO	DEADLINE	DONE

HANUKKAH TO DO LIST

TO DO	DEADLINE	DONE

HANUKKAH TO DO LIST

TO DO	DEADLINE	DONE

HANUKKAH TO DO LIST

TO DO	DEADLINE	DONE

HANUKKAH TO DO LIST

TO DO	DEADLINE	DONE

HANUKKAH TO DO LIST

TO DO	DEADLINE	DONE

HANUKKAH CARD LIST

NAME	ADDRESS	SENT

HANUKKAH CARD LIST

NAME	ADDRESS	SENT

HANUKKAH CARD LIST

NAME	ADDRESS	SENT

HANUKKAH CARD LIST

NAME	ADDRESS	SENT

HANUKKAH CARD LIST

NAME	ADDRESS	SENT

HANUKKAH CARD LIST

NAME	ADDRESS	SENT

HANUKKAH CARD LIST

NAME	ADDRESS	SENT

HANUKKAH CARD LIST

NAME	ADDRESS	SENT

HANUKKAH CARD LIST

NAME	ADDRESS	SENT

HANUKKAH CARD LIST

NAME	ADDRESS	SENT

HANUKKAH SHOPPING LIST

NAME	GIFT	WHERE TO FIND	PRICE

HANUKKAH SHOPPING LIST

NAME	GIFT	WHERE TO FIND	PRICE

HANUKKAH SHOPPING LIST

NAME	GIFT	WHERE TO FIND	PRICE

HANUKKAH SHOPPING LIST

NAME	GIFT	WHERE TO FIND	PRICE

HANUKKAH SHOPPING LIST

NAME	GIFT	WHERE TO FIND	PRICE

HANUKKAH SHOPPING LIST

NAME	GIFT	WHERE TO FIND	PRICE

HANUKKAH SHOPPING LIST

NAME	GIFT	WHERE TO FIND	PRICE

HANUKKAH SHOPPING LIST

NAME	GIFT	WHERE TO FIND	PRICE

HANUKKAH SHOPPING LIST

NAME	GIFT	WHERE TO FIND	PRICE

HANUKKAH SHOPPING LIST

NAME	GIFT	WHERE TO FIND	PRICE

8 CRAZY NIGHTS

THURSDAY

FRIDAY

SATURDAY

SUNDAY

MONDAY

TUESDAY

WEDNESDAY

THURSDAY

FRIDAY

SATURDAY

SUNDAY

MONDAY

TUESDAY

WEDNESDAY

NOTES

NOTES

NOTES

NOTES

NOTES

NOTES

NOTES

NOTES

NOTES

NOTES

NOTES

NOTES

NOTES

NOTES

NOTES

NOTES

NOTES

NOTES

NOTES

NOTES

NOTES

NOTES

NOTES

NOTES

NOTES

NOTES

NOTES

NOTES

NOTES

NOTES

NOTES

NOTES

NOTES

NOTES

NOTES

NOTES

NOTES

NOTES

NOTES

NOTES

NOTES

NOTES

NOTES

NOTES

NOTES

NOTES

NOTES

NOTES

NOTES

NOTES

NOTES

NOTES

NOTES

NOTES

NOTES

NOTES

NOTES

NOTES

NOTES

NOTES

NOTES

NOTES

NOTES

NOTES

NOTES

NOTES

NOTES

NOTES

NOTES

NOTES

NOTES

NOTES

NOTES

NOTES

NOTES

Made in the USA
Lexington, KY
29 November 2018